EYEWITNESS TO THE
LIBERATION OF
BUCHENWALD

BY JILL SHERMAN

Published by The Child's World®
1980 Lookout Drive • Mankato, MN 56003-1705
800-599-READ • www.childsworld.com

Acknowledgments
The Child's World®: Mary Berendes, Publishing Director
Red Line Editorial: Design, editorial direction, and production
Photographs ©: Byron Rollins/AP Images, cover, 1; Deutsche Fotothek/DPA/Corbis,
4; Ira Nowinski/Corbis, 7, 16; Everett Historical/Shutterstock Images, 8, 10, 13, 14, 19;
Shutterstock Images, 20, 23; AP Images, 24, 27; Picture-Alliance/DPA/AP Images, 25;
adoc-photos/Corbis, 28

ISBN 9781634074179

LCCN 2015946229

Printed in the United States of America
Mankato, MN
December, 2015
PA02281

ABOUT THE AUTHOR

Jill Sherman lives and writes in Brooklyn, New York. She has written more
than a dozen books for young readers. Sherman believes it is important to
remember the past and honor those who have suffered.

TABLE OF
CONTENTS

Chapter 1

LIBERATION DAY

On April 11, 1945, the forests in central Germany were quiet. Troops and vehicles of the U.S. Third Army were traveling through the trees. Private Harry J. Herder was on alert. His division had been told to investigate Buchenwald, a German war camp. However, most of the men knew little about their assignment.

At the time, Germany was controlled by the **Nazi Party**. The country was part of a group of nations called the Axis Powers. They had been at war with the Allied Powers since 1939. The Allied Powers included Britain, the United States, and the Soviet Union.

The American troops neared the camp. Their tanks slowed down but did not stop. They crashed through barbed-wire fences. Soldiers jumped to the ground. They prepared to meet enemy troops. But no attack came.

Something wasn't right. The camp was eerily quiet. A pillar of foul-smelling black smoke poured from a chimney. Soldiers examined the buildings around them. They looked for people nearby.

An iron gate into Buchenwald read *Jedem das Seine*. In English, this means "to give each person what he or she deserves." But what did that message mean? Why was it in a war camp?

The soldiers moved forward with caution. Most carried rifles, ready for an attack. But then the soldiers spotted some movement. "A ragged group of human beings started to creep out of and from between the buildings in front of us," Private Herder recalled. "They came out of the buildings and just stood there, making me feel foolish with all of that firepower hanging on me. I certainly wouldn't be needing it with these folks."[1]

> "When we heard noises at about a quarter past three, we looked out of the window—which took a great effort—and one of my friends said with a weak voice, 'I think we are getting liberated.' And we thought he had lost his sense of reality like so many people there."
>
> —Henry Oster, a Buchenwald survivor[2]

Men from the camp slowly shuffled forward. They were weak and thin. Ribs showed through their pale skin. Their dark, sunken eyes revealed their suffering. But there was something else in their eyes, too. Soon, the men learned that the soldiers were American. Relief and joy spread through the crowd. The Americans had arrived to **liberate** them.

Buchenwald was a **concentration camp**. Many prisoners were Jewish. The camp also housed other people whom the Nazi Party deemed "unwanteds." Buchenwald held military prisoners and criminals. Roma (also known as

The gates to Buchenwald read *Jedem das Seine*, "to give each ▶ person what he or she deserves."

▲ **Adolf Hitler, leader of Nazi Germany, introduced brutal policies against Jews.**

gypsies) and Jehovah's Witnesses were also sent to the camp. At one time, Buchenwald held inmates from 51 nations. These prisoners were denied meals or fed only thin soups. They were forced to work long hours at grueling tasks. By the time the

Americans arrived, most prisoners were starving. Some were too weak to leave their bunks.

Buchenwald was not the only place like this. The Nazis had 20,000 concentration camps. These camps were not discovered until 1945. But Nazis had been using the camps for years. Their first camp, Dachau, opened in 1933. That was shortly after the Nazis came into power.

The Nazi Party had gained support in Germany because many Germans wanted change. In 1918, Germany surrendered in World War I. As a result, the country lost power in the world. Germans faced poverty or struggled to find work. The Nazis promised they would return Germany to power. Many Germans rallied behind Adolf Hitler, the leader of the Nazi Party. Hitler blamed Germany's problems on Jews. Soon, **anti-Semitism** had taken hold in the country.

In 1933, Hitler was named the chancellor of Germany. He used his position to strengthen Nazi power. The **Schutzstaffel**, or SS, served as part of the Nazi Party's military force. They enforced Nazi laws. Often, they attacked Jews or destroyed their property.

Hitler's supporters painted hateful slogans in Jewish cemeteries. Students and teachers burned books by Jewish authors. Many Jews feared for their lives. But conditions would soon be even worse.

Chapter 2

FEAR AND VIOLENCE

During the 1930s, Jews lost their rights as citizens of Germany. Other Germans were told to avoid Jewish-owned businesses. Hanne Hirsch, a Jewish child in the city of Karlsruhe, lost many friends. "They could no longer associate with me," she remembered. "I would not dare associate with them."[3]

In 1933, officials painted the word "Jew" on the Hirsch family's store. This was a warning to other Germans to stay away.

In 1938, many Jewish immigrants were ordered to leave Germany. They were given one night to leave. Desperate people crammed their belongings into one suitcase, all they were allowed to take. Nazi officials seized the rest of their possessions.

Herschel Grynszpan was a young Jewish man whose parents had to leave their home. He was furious about the Nazis' cruel actions. On November 7, 1938, Grynszpan entered a German embassy building in Paris. In his anger, he shot and killed a German diplomat. In his pocket, he carried a folded postcard. He had written on it, "My dear parents, I could not do otherwise. . . . The heart bleeds when I hear of your tragedy."[4]

This murder deeply angered many Germans. Joseph Goebbels was a powerful Nazi official. He urged Nazi followers to attack Jews. Riots erupted in many Jewish neighborhoods. Goebbels told the SS not to interfere. He said, "A Jew has fired a shot. A German has died. Obviously our people will be outraged about this. This is not the time to rein in that outrage."[5]

The rioters caused incredible destruction across Germany. They burned **synagogues**. They barged into Jewish homes. They smashed windows of Jewish-owned shops. Siegfried Merecki remembered, "Every little thing that was still inside was taken out and smashed to pieces. The floor was torn up. The people seemed to have superhuman strength."[6] The name given to these riots is *Kristallnacht*. It means "Night of Broken Glass."

Nazi leaders were happy with the damage *Kristallnacht* had caused. In two days, 250 synagogues had been destroyed. Thousands of Jewish businesses were looted. Hundreds of Jews were injured. At least 96 were dead. The riots showed the Nazis they had the support of most German citizens. Goebbels wanted to start removing the Jews from Germany.

Officials began forcing Jews to live in **ghettos**. In Theresienstadt, Jews marched through grassy hills to reach the ghetto gates. Brick walls trapped them inside. Armed guards watched over them from a high tower. In 1939, Nazi armies

"I saw much suffering around me. The ghetto was very overcrowded. . . . From our windows I could see the inside of the ghetto wall."

—*Ed Herman, a Jewish man who lived in a ghetto in Warsaw, Poland*[7]

▲ A concrete wall was built around the Jewish ghetto in Warsaw, Poland.

invaded Poland and Czechoslovakia. These invasions led to the beginning of World War II. Jews in invaded countries also had to live in ghettos.

After the Jews moved to ghettos, officers began to round them up and take them away. At first, no one knew what was happening. Karl Schwabe was confused when the Nazi officials came to his door. "They refused to explain the grounds for my arrest," he remembered. "I had a clear conscience and tried to console my wife . . . then I followed the officers."[8] SS men forced men like Schwabe onto crowded trains. They suffered for days with no food or water. The train brought them to Buchenwald concentration camp.

Chapter 3

PRISON LIFE

On a winter day in 1938, men struggled on a path to Buchenwald. The group included Jews and other prisoners. Despite the cold weather, they were sweating. Guards shouted at the men to hurry. Fierce dogs accompanied them. The guards swiftly punished prisoners who disobeyed. They shot one man for stopping to tie his shoes. "This is how we arrive at Buchenwald—

in a state of total and utter exhaustion," wrote one prisoner, Jack Werber.[9]

Buchenwald had opened on July 15, 1937. By the next day, the first 300 prisoners had arrived at the camp. At first, all of the prisoners were men. Immediately, they were put to work. Men were forced to haul boulders for ten hours a day. Even sick or elderly men had to work.

The camp soon became severely overcrowded. Prisoners slept in sheep pens. As the camp population grew, Nazis forced prisoners to construct housing for the new inmates. But because the men had few materials for building, the housing provided little protection from the weather. Barracks buildings were made of shoddy wooden boards. They had no floors. Men slept on tiny bunks or on the bare, muddy ground. All night, Karl Schwabe heard screams and cries from other prisoners. In the morning, he and the other prisoners were forced to stand for hours. Sick prisoners fell and were harshly punished.

As the camp grew, so did the kinds of people who were sent there. The Nazis shipped political enemies to Buchenwald. **Satellite camps** began to take female prisoners in 1943 or 1944. Like the men, they were forced to work all day.

In summer 1944, Eva Pusztai was sent to the satellite camp of Muenchmuehle. Women at the camp worked up to 15 hours a day. Each day, Pusztai risked starvation and sickness. "You got just enough food to survive," she remembered. "I lost a third of my weight and I was almost starving to death."[10] Trigger-ready guards shot prisoners who could not work quickly enough.

Nazi doctors also worked at Buchenwald. SS guards selected prisoners. The guards took them to a cold hospital-like setting in Block 46 of the camp. Even prisoners who had not seen this area were frightened of it. "Every man in the camp knew that Block 46 was a dreadful place," recalled prisoner Eügen Kogon.[11]

At first, the thin, dirty inmates did not know exactly why doctors wanted them. They might have hoped for medical care. But the prisoners received only a quick examination and an injection. They would return for more exams and more injections. The prisoners did not know it, but the doctors were giving them infections and diseases. Then the doctors tried out untested vaccines on the prisoners. Kogon watched in horror as other prisoners rapidly became ill. "People would refuse to eat, and a large [number] of them would die," he remembered.[12]

But the experiments did not stop there. In the winter, groups of prisoners were stripped naked. Guards doused them with

◀ **Guards watched Buchenwald prisoners from a high tower.**

> "The first days were the worst. We were made to go thirsty. Water was in short supply and none of it was given to us. . . . When on the third day bread was distributed, I couldn't get it down."
>
> —*Karl E. Schwabe, describing his time at Buchenwald*[14]

water. Then they made the inmates stand in the snow. Prisoners could not go inside until they were nearly dead from the cold. "They were then trundled into the hospital, and every effort was made to revive them," said Private Harry Herder, who helped liberate the camp. "Every effort failed."[13] The experiment was to find cures for a condition called hypothermia. The experiment was repeated again and again. But the prisoners continued to die.

Fighting back was dangerous. However, some men formed a **resistance** movement. Most had been sent to Buchenwald as political prisoners. Members of the resistance protected each other. Some also looked out for other prisoners. Wilhelm Hamman, a resistance leader, kept young children safe. He helped the children remove patches on their clothes identifying them as Jewish. Because Jews were treated worse than other prisoners, this action may have saved their lives.

▲ **Nazis seized prisoners' possessions, including their gold wedding rings.**

Many of the political prisoners knew about certain skills or trades. As a result, some resistance workers had important jobs at the camp. Their jobs gave them certain benefits. They wore leather jackets, while other prisoners had only coarse, thin garments. The close-knit resistance members looked out for each other. They shared clothing and food with friends. However they could, prisoners tried to make life at the camp more bearable.

Chapter 4

DEATH MARCH

In January 1945, thousands of prisoners marched in snow and cold. These prisoners were walking to Buchenwald from other concentration camps. They tramped through the snow wearing only rags. For weeks, prisoners walked for many miles every day. They were allowed to sleep only for a few hours at a time.

The tide of the war was turning. Soviet troops were advancing in Europe. The Germans were fighting to protect their land. Their eastern concentration camps were threatened. SS leaders ordered these camps to transfer prisoners to Buchenwald.

This "death march" lasted for months. In the brutal cold of winter, prisoners traveled by foot, train, truck, or boat. They had even fewer supplies than prisoners had at the camps. SS guards shot those who could not keep up. Thousands were left behind. They died from exposure, starvation, and exhaustion.

Those who survived the trip were near death by the end of it. "How pitiful is the state of these new arrivals!" said prisoner Avraham Gottlieb. "Many corpses were removed from the cars, and many are ill. The healthy are painfully thin."[15] Each day, the camp became more crowded.

Yet the new prisoners would not remain at Buchenwald for long. Soviet, American, and British troops were on the march. German troops were retreating. In early April, SS officers received a message: Allied soldiers are closing in. Evacuate Buchenwald immediately!

SS officers raced to follow this order. They crowded prisoners onto trains out of camp. Many were sick or starving. They knew they could not survive the journey. The Buchenwald resistance tried to delay the evacuation. They disobeyed orders, risking punishment from guards. They knew that if the Allies reached the camp, they would be freed. In the end, the SS sent 28,000 prisoners out of the main camp. But tens of thousands of prisoners remained at Buchenwald.

The prisoners knew that something important was happening. Each day a group left the camp. And each day the prisoners heard gunfire approaching closer. Eventually, most SS guards abandoned the camp. They left 21,000 prisoners behind.

Resistance members desperately sought help. They had secretly built a radio to communicate with people outside the camp. On April 8, 1945, they sent out a message in three languages: English, German, and Russian. "To the Allies," the message began. "To the army of General Patton. This is the Buchenwald concentration camp. SOS. We request help."[16] No response came. But resistance members were still hopeful. They repeated the message.

Barbed-wire fences surrounded the Buchenwald ▶ concentration camp.

Chapter 5

WAR CRIMES

Resistance members listened anxiously for a reply to their plea. A few minutes later, they received a return message. "Hold out," came the reply. "Rushing to your aid. Staff of Third Army."[17] One prisoner fainted from surprise.

Finally, on April 11, 1945, American tanks arrived at the camp. "From every corner of the camp we could hear the announcement over American

loudspeakers," remembered Yechezkel Tydor. The announcement
said *Ihr seid frei*, "You are free." Tydor said, "This was the day of
our liberation."[18]

▲ After Buchenwald was liberated, children from the camp
were taken to a hospital for treatment.

From 1937 to 1945, about 240,000 people had been held in Buchenwald. American soldiers liberated 21,000 prisoners. The other prisoners had been evacuated or killed at the camp.

U.S. Generals George Patton and Dwight D. Eisenhower arrived to inspect the camp. They were alarmed by what they found. The starving prisoners, filthy beds, and tiny living spaces showed the horror of what had happened. Army officials found bodies of prisoners who had died. Patton ordered residents of the nearest town to march to Buchenwald. He wanted them to see what had been happening all around them.

According to Private Harry Herder, Patton "wanted every citizen . . . to see what the German people were responsible for. The engineers were not to bury the dead until after the grand tour by the German townspeople."[19] The citizens obeyed Patton's

"They had these thin pajama clothes, they had terrible food, you can imagine. . . . They were so afraid of authority that they were very careful about speaking to us, but they were so hungry that they dared, and that was such an act of courage, I think, for them to speak to us."

—*Private Robert Harmon, U.S. Third Army*[20]

▲ **Citizens of a nearby German town viewed the
concentration camp.**

order. Most had known that concentration camps existed. But
they were horrified by what they saw. Some wept as they viewed
the weak, ill survivors.

Meanwhile, the German army was on the run. They knew they
were losing the war. On May 7, 1945, Germany surrendered to
the Allies. The war in Europe had finally come to an end. Allied

troops freed more concentration camps. People around the world learned how the prisoners had been treated. Though terrible things often happen in war, what happened to the prisoners was far worse. Those responsible would need to be punished.

The Allies charged Nazi leaders with crimes against peace, **war crimes**, and crimes against humanity. They would hold a trial, the first of its kind. The Allied countries each supplied a judge. The Nuremberg Trials would decide the fate of the Nazi leaders. The trials began on November 20, 1945.

Nearly one year later, the judges decided their verdicts. Twelve Nazi leaders were sentenced to death. Seven others received prison sentences. Only three were found not guilty.

But the trials were only a first step. The Allies wanted to make sure that something like this never happened again. On October 24, 1945, 51 countries founded the United Nations. Today, more than 140 nations have joined. Through the organization, nations work together for peace and human rights.

Concentration camps showed the worst side of humanity. The Nazis murdered millions of people. No one stopped them. Today, nations are united against those terrible crimes. They make efforts never to let people suffer like that again.

◄ **Nazi officials listened to the evidence against them during the Nuremberg Trials.**

GLOSSARY

anti-Semitism (an-tee-SEM-i-ti-zum): Discrimination against or hatred of Jewish people is called anti-Semitism. Jewish people faced anti-Semitism during World War II.

concentration camp (kon-suhn-TREY-shuhn KAMP): In a concentration camp, people are imprisoned and sometimes killed. Buchenwald was a large concentration camp.

ghettos (GET-ohz): Ghettos are parts of a city where certain people are forced to live. The Nazis forced Jews into ghettos.

liberate (LIB-uh-rayt): To liberate is to set free. Prisoners at Buchenwald sent messages so the Allies could liberate them.

Nazi Party (NAHT-see PAR-tee): The Nazi Party controlled Germany from 1933 to 1945. The Nazi Party introduced brutal laws against Jews.

resistance (ri-ZIS-tuns): A resistance is a secret group that fights back against people in power. The resistance at Buchenwald tried to make life better for prisoners.

satellite camps (SAT-i-lahyt KAMPS): Satellite camps are smaller prison camps connected to a main concentration camp. Buchenwald contained many satellite camps.

Schutzstaffel (SHOOTS-shta-ful): The Schutzstaffel, or SS, was a Nazi military group. Some Schutzstaffel units ran concentration camps.

synagogues (SIN-uh-gogz): Synagogues are places where Jewish people hold religious services. Nazis destroyed many synagogues.

war crimes (wawr krahymz): War crimes are cruel acts committed in wartime. The Nuremberg Trials investigated Nazi war crimes.

SOURCE NOTES

1. Harry J. Herder, Jr. "The Liberation of Buchenwald." *A People's History of the Holocaust and Genocide*. Remember.org, n.d. Web. 20 July 2015.

2. Dorothee Thiesing. "Nazi Concentration Camp Survivors Mark 70th Anniversary of Buchenwald Liberation." *The Huffington Post*. Huffington Post.com, Inc., 11 April 2015. Web. 20 July 2015.

3. "Oral History: Hanne Hirsch Liebmann." *The Holocaust: A Learning Site for Students*. United States Holocaust Memorial Museum, n.d. Web. 20 July 2015.

4. Saul S. Friedman. *A History of the Holocaust*. Portland, OR: Vallentine Mitchell, 2004. Print. 85.

5. David Irving. "Revelations from Goebbels' Diary." *Journal of Historical Review*. Institute for Historical Review, January/February 1995. Web. 24 July 2015.

6. Uta Gerhardt and Thomas Karlauf. *The Night of Broken Glass: Eyewitness Accounts of Kristallnacht*. Cambridge, UK: Polity Press. Print. 37.

7. Ed Herman. "My Warsaw Ghetto Memories." *Frontline*. WGBH Educational Foundation, 14 May 2013. Web. 24 July 2015.

8. Uta Gerhardt and Thomas Karlauf. 96.

9. Jack Werber and William B. Helmreich. *Saving Children: Diary of a Buchenwald Survivor and Rescuer*. Piscataway, NJ: Transaction Publishers, 2014. Print. 1–2.

10. Lisi Niesner. "Holocaust Survivors Remember the Horrors of Buchenwald." *NBC News Photo Blog*. NBC News, 16 April 2013. Web. 20 July 2015.

11-12. James M. Glass. *Life Unworthy of Life: Racial Phobia and Mass Murder in Hitler's Germany*. New York: Basic Books, 1997. Print. 93.

13. Harry J. Herder, Jr. n.d.

14. Uta Gerhardt and Thomas Karlauf. 99.

15. Judith Tydor Baumel. *Kibbutz Buchenwald: Survivors and Prisoners*. New Brunswick, NJ: Rutgers UP, 1997. Print. 6.

16-17. Ian Buruma. *Year Zero: A History of 1945*. New York: Penguin, 2013. Print. 241.

18. Judith Tydor Baumel. 7.

19. Harry J. Herder, Jr. n.d.

20. Dorothee Thiesing. 11 April 2015.

TO LEARN MORE

Books

Adams, Simon. *World War II*. New York: DK Publishing, 2014.

Downing, David. *The Nazi Death Camps*. New York: Gareth Stevens, 2005.

Warren, Andrea. *Surviving Hitler: A Boy in the Nazi Death Camps*. New York: Harper Collins, 2013.

Web Sites

Visit our Web site for links about the liberation of Buchenwald: childsworld.com/links

Note to Parents, Teachers, and Librarians: We routinely verify our Web links to make sure they are safe and active sites. So encourage your readers to check them out!

INDEX